A STAY-AT-HOME DAD'S GUIDE
— TO —
PRESCHOOL NUTRITION

DR. JON KESTER

authorHOUSE®

AuthorHouse™
1663 Liberty Drive
Bloomington, IN 47403
www.authorhouse.com
Phone: 1 (800) 839-8640

Disclaimer: Before implementing any of the advice, tips, and strategies found in this book, be sure to get your physician's consent.

Published by AuthorHouse 10/15/2019

ISBN: 978-1-7283-3183-6 (sc)
ISBN: 978-1-7283-3182-9 (e)

Print information available on the last page.

Any people depicted in stock imagery provided by Getty Images are models, and such images are being used for illustrative purposes only. Certain stock imagery © Getty Images.

This book is printed on acid-free paper.

To Nanna Sharon, who thinks that all I feed my kids is soda pop and potato chips. Read this book, and you will find out the truth!

CONTENTS

Introduction

This book aims to create future healthier generations through good nutrition and empower parents with the goal of helping their preschooler reach his or her full potential.

In the twenty-first century, it is very easy to get confused about how, what, and when to feed your preschooler. Between the news, blogs, and social media, it's easy to feel overwhelmed with all the different messages. This book will give parents a straightforward, informative, and simple approach to nutrition for preschoolers.

First, all parents must remember that preschoolers are not babies anymore and are small people who need the same nutrients adults do. They need protein, fat, and carbohydrates just like us. So in that sense, feeding preschoolers is simple: give them all the nutritious foods you already eat and know to be healthy. Parents also need to remember that nutrition affects all aspects of childhood growth, development, and health, which includes maintaining a healthy weight; avoiding health problems related to excess body fat, and brain development.

As parents we must keep in mind that once a body is overweight at a critical developmental period, it's very hard to change. Health and physical activity habits established in early life could have lasting effects for decades to come.

Nutrition Problems Facing Preschoolers

Today, more than anytime in history, preschoolers face health issues based on being overweight or obese. According to the Department of Health and Human Services statics in 1980, only 5 percent of American kids aged two to four were obese. In 2010, it was 19 percent—nearly one in five. Now, in 2018, about 40 percent of US preschoolers are classified as overweight or obese.

Health problems overweight preschoolers can face

Excess body fat that exists on overweight preschoolers isn't healthy, and it sets the stage for both childhood and adult diseases. Here is a list of some of the health conditions that may occur later in life due to being overweight or obese:

- **Cardiovascular disease.** Eighty percent of obese teens are already showing signs of cardiovascular disease—a health problem that normally doesn't appear until decades later (Sellen 2001).
- **Asthma.** Adipose tissue (fat) secretes hormones and chemical signals; too much fat means inflammation. In kids, this means things like asthma. A Mayo clinic study (2016) found that there has been a 30 percent increase in childhood asthma over the last ten years.
- **Liver disease.** Fat can accumulate in the liver; nonalcoholic fatty liver disease (NAFLD) is the leading cause of liver disease in kids in the United States (Terras 1994). Children with fatty livers face double the risk of arterial plaque buildup.
- **Diabetes.** Overweight children have impaired insulin sensitivity and glucose disposal, which leads to diabetes (Werbach 1989).
- **Cancer/Chronic disease.** Overweight children have a higher long-term risk of chronic conditions such as stroke;

breast, colon, and kidney cancers; musculoskeletal disorders; and gall bladder disease (Werbach 1989).

Mental health and being overweight

Extra body fat for a child is not only a physical health concern but also a psychosocial burden too. It's no fun being the chubby kid on the playground who has a hard time running and playing. Overweight and obese kids and teens face teasing and social exclusion.

Obese children in many cases are more likely to have low self-esteem than their thinner peers (Galloway 2006). Weak self-esteem can translate into feelings of shame about their body, and lack of self-confidence can lead to poorer academic performance at school down the road. Over time, obese children who feel they do not fit in or don't belong can also become clinically depressed and withdrawn.

The Beginning to a Healthier Preschooler

The issue of good childhood nutrition may seem overwhelming at first, especially if you're a parent trying to make healthier choices for yourself and your family. The big question this book answers is: Where to begin? In the following chapters, parents will be informed on the following topics:

- taking the lead as a parent and becoming a role model;
- the proper portion sizes for preschoolers;
- the best and worst foods that preschoolers can eat;
- supplementing foods with vitamins and minerals;
- how to deal with picky eaters; and
- sample healthy menus.

CHAPTER 1

PARENTS AS ROLE MODELS

Children are born without knowledge of proper nutrition and the skills to make healthy choices, and in most cases, they eagerly look for someone to imitate. That someone is usually one or both parents. Parents are a child's first teachers and role models. Remember that children are more affected by what their parents do than by what their parents say. Preschoolers learn how to behave by seeing how their mothers and fathers behave and by following their example. A preschooler learns good nutrition habits more easily when parents make good nutrition a part of daily life.

One of the best ways to halt obesity for the next generation is through parents being good role models for their children in the areas of nutrition and lifestyle. The ways parents talk about food, cook meals, and eat are the most important influences for developing a child's healthy eating habits. According to a study by the Nebraska Department of Health and Human Services (2015), children watch and imitate adults for everything from saying please and thank you to engaging in fitness and nutrition behavior. It is not enough for parents to just teach healthy eating habits to children. Children must see parents practicing what they are teaching. Parents, you must eat the way you want your children to eat.

Healthy role-model parents need to make sure to do the following:

- Communicate with children and stay active in monitoring what they eat. Take the time to listen and share their concerns about certain foods. Practice healthy eating habits, such as drinking water and milk instead of soda, energy drinks, and alcohol. Also, parents need to limit junk food in the house and avoid going out to eat.
- Be knowledgeable and well-rounded about healthy eating. Great role models aren't just teachers. They are constant learners who challenge themselves to get out of their comfort zones. This may be tied to always eating breakfast, lunch, and dinner or eating smaller portion sizes. When preschoolers see that their parents can eat and be healthy, they will learn to be successful.
- Make a commitment to a healthy lifestyle. Parents need to make sure their preschoolers know expectations of nutritional eating and hold both themselves and the children accountable for actions.
- Show teamwork. Parents as role models also need to make meals a team effort by having kids help prepare meals, set the table, and help with cleanup. The basic skills of cooking and eating healthy will resonate for a lifetime and can be passed down to future generations. We as parents must give our children the knowledge and tools to end the obesity epidemic. The best way to learn proper eating habits is by looking at strategies that work and don't work and then applying them to everyday life.

Strategies That *Don't* Work

There are countless strategies that parents have used with their preschoolers over the years to try to get them to have a healthier diet. The fact is that most of these so-called strategies do not work and can actually lead to negative effects that prevent families from reaching the ultimate goal of proper nutrition. Here are some strategies to stay away from:

- Don't offer preschoolers food as a reward when they're upset. "If you stop crying, you can have a sucker."
- Don't have too strict rules about "good" and "bad" foods. "No cookies allowed in our house We only eat oatmeal for breakfast."
- Don't push preschoolers to clean their plates.
- Don't bribe preschoolers with unhealthy foods to eat healthy "If you finish your spinach, you'll get ice cream."

Unfortunately, the strategies above have an undesirable effect on your preschooler's nutrition. Try to follow the strategies below instead, and watch your preschooler's nutrition radically improve.

Healthy Eating Strategies That Work

- Serve appropriate portions.
- Serve a balanced selection of healthy, unprocessed whole foods.
- Don't keep unhealthy choices in the house.
- Make sure preschoolers are getting all their proper vitamins and minerals.
- Let preschoolers stop eating when they're no longer hungry instead of insisting that they clean their plates.
- Involve kids in menu planning, shopping, and cooking.
- Eat together as a family as often as possible; make mealtime family time.

The next chapter of this book will go into more detail on how to implement these strategies.

CHAPTER 2

SPECIFIC EATING STRATEGIES

Strategy 1: Serve Appropriate Portions

Preschoolers need the same variety of nutrient-rich foods as older children and adults, just in smaller portions. However, as portions have gotten bigger for adults, some parents and caregivers have developed a distorted view of the amount of food toddlers and preschoolers need. In many cases, preschoolers have as much food on their plates as adults, which is simply too much. The biggest mistake most parents make is thinking that their children are not eating enough and insisting kids eat more than they need. The result of parents giving children portions that are too large or expecting them to clean their plates is that the children may become overweight or obese.

The United States is facing a health crisis related to obesity. An alarming statistic from a 2017 study by the Centers for Disease Control and Prevention is that 22 percent of children starting school are either overweight or obese. One of the main reasons has been an increase in portion sizes. A U.S. Department of Agriculture (2016) children's health and wellness study found that some portion sizes are now double what they were twenty years ago.

According to the USDA dietary guidelines (2017), an appropriate serving size for children two to three years of age is about half an adult serving. Most two- to three-year-old children need to consume about one thousand to twelve hundred calories per day. Here's how to distribute those calories in a healthy eating plan:

- **Grains.** About three to four ounces of grains per day, preferably half of them whole grains. That means one or two slices of bread plus one cup of ready-to-eat cereal and half a cup of cooked rice or pasta.
- **Vegetables.** One to one and a half cups of raw or cooked vegetables per day. Like adults, young kids need variety, such as mashed sweet potatoes, broccoli with low-fat dip, and tomato sauce for pasta.
- **Fruits.** One cup of fresh, frozen, canned, or dried fruit per day. Limit juice to four to six ounces per day. Emphasize whole fruits rather than juice. Kids love melon balls, mandarin oranges (fresh or canned in juice), and frozen berries.
- **Milk.** Two to two and a half cups per day. Whole milk is recommended for children younger than two. Older children can have lower-fat, calcium-rich choices, such as fat-free or low-fat milk, yogurt, and cheese.
- **Meats and beans.** Two to three ounces total per day. Options include lean meat, poultry, fish, one egg, cooked beans (e.g., black, pinto, and kidney), and peanut butter.

One reason kids may not be eating appropriately sized portions is because parents and caregivers may not recognize what a reasonable portion looks like. Many times in the past when I've given seminars on nutrition, people have asked, "What does one-half cup of rice look like? What about four ounces of chicken or two tablespoons of peanut butter?" Instead of having to carry around measuring cups and scales, it's easier to compare portion sizes to everyday household items. An example of this would be to imagine one cup as the size of a baseball. Before serving your children food or drink, you can think of the relevant object and choose a portion that matches its size.

Parents, remember that food amounts given to preschoolers should fall into the *recommended ranges* rather than *specific amounts* since young children have fluctuating appetites and tend to eat more at some meals and less at others. Parents can use the portion sizes as a guide on how much to offer to their young children; however, they should then allow children to eat according to their appetite. Keep in mind that taller or more active children will eat larger portions than shorter or less active children. Parents must not urge young children to finish everything on the plate or to eat more than they want to.

Note: The amount of food and number of servings children need daily from each food group depends on their age and how active they are. Some parents worry because young children seem to eat small amounts of food, especially when compared with adult portions. Remember, a child who is growing well is getting enough to eat. If you are concerned, talk with your child's doctor.

Strategy 2: Serve a Balanced Selection of Healthy, Unprocessed Whole Foods

A preschooler's eating plan should consist mostly of healthy foods with a balance of protein, carbohydrates, and healthy fats. According to the USDA dietary guidelines(2017), a recommendation for each of these nutrients is 40 percent carbohydrates, 30 percent protein, and no more than 13 percent from fat.

Here is an at-a-glance guide to the main food types that should be included in your child's diet:

Carbohydrates

This group should make up the largest part (around 40 percent) of your child's diet. Bread, rice, fruits, and vegetables are the body's main source of energy and provide vitamins, minerals, and fiber. Carbohydrates are also a good source of iron, which is essential for forming red blood cells that carry oxygen around the body. A good intake of iron is also necessary for energy, intellectual performance, and vitality.

Try to choose whole-grain carbohydrates, such as brown rice or bread, rather than white bread or rice. Whole-grain carbohydrates release sugar relatively slowly into the bloodstream, which helps provide long-lasting energy. Also, refined carbohydrates like white bread have lost many of their valuable nutrients during processing.

Fruits and vegetables are also important parts of carbohydrates as they provide vitamins and minerals that help protect against cancer and heart disease. Root vegetables in particular are an important carbohydrate for energy.

Recommended daily intake. Preschoolers between one and three years old should eat about four servings of grain-based carbohydrates each day. One serving is one slice of bread, a small portion of brown rice or pasta, or a small bowl of cereal. Children should also eat four to five servings of carbs in the form of fruits and vegetables. This could include half an apple, four dried apricots, a tablespoon of peas, and one tomato.

Protein

Protein is very important for preschoolers since it is one of the most important nutrients for the growth, maintenance, and repair of body tissue. Red meat provides the best and most easily absorbed source of iron as well, which is something that most preschoolers do not get enough of. Not getting enough protein can also lower resistance to infection.

Most preschoolers' main source of protein is dairy. Dairy foods provide not only protein but also vitamins and minerals and are the best source of calcium. Calcium is very important for bone and teeth health of young children.

Recommended daily intake. Preschoolers should eat meat or chicken three to four times a week. Protein foods like cheese or eggs are a good source for breakfast. Children should have three portions of milk or dairy products each day. This could be a glass of milk, a cup of yogurt, or a few pieces of cheese.

Fats

Healthy fats should make up 8 to 13 percent of a preschooler's diet. Healthy fats come in the form of fish, milk, nuts, and seeds and are critical for brain development and visual development. Including healthy fats in a preschooler's diet may help to improve the performance of children with learning difficulties as well.

Recommended daily intake. Preschoolers should eat healthy fats three to four times a week.

Examples of healthy foods that every preschooler should eat

- **Eggs** offer protein, and they're one of the few foods that naturally contain vitamin D, which helps the body absorb calcium. Eating protein at breakfast helps kids feel satisfied longer.
- **Yogurt** gives preschoolers plenty of good bacteria, also known as probiotics, which are key to keeping little stomachs happy and healthy. Be sure to limit sugary versions aimed at kids because these are often lower in protein and good bacteria. Instead, choose plain nonfat or low-fat yogurt or Greek yogurt. Look for the words "live and active cultures" on the carton to ensure that the yogurt has plenty of beneficial bacteria.
- **Flaxseed** is a nutty plant food that is packed full of omega-3 fatty acids. Omega-3 is needed for optimal brain development. Flaxseed is sold whole and ground, but research suggests that ground is absorbed by the body better. Try sprinkling ground flaxseed onto cereal or into the batter of pancakes or waffles. Replace one-quarter cup of flour

with ground flaxseed in your child's favorite muffin, bread, or cupcake recipe to add a healthy boost to baked goods.

- **Sweet potato** is one of the most nutritious (and inexpensive) vegetables around. The vitamin A in sweet potatoes keeps eyes healthy and acts like an antioxidant in the body. Sweet potatoes are a favorite among preschool children because of their natural sweetness and bright color, but they are often forgotten once kids get older. Try a baked sweet potato the next time you need a side dish. Simply wash, pierce with a fork, and bake at 375 degrees for forty-five minutes or until tender.

- **Black beans** are a great source of protein, as well as fiber and calcium—two things kids tend not to get enough of. The best ways to get preschoolers to eat these beans is by making nachos or quesadillas with black beans, cheese, and salsa.

- **Mango** is a sweet tropical fruit that will provide your preschooler with almost a whole day's supply of vitamin C in just one fruit. The vitamin C helps keep kids' immune systems running strong and keeps teeth and gums healthy. It also provides three grams of fiber for just around one hundred calories. Buy fresh or jarred in juice to serve cut up or in a smoothie or dessert like banana-mango smoothie or double mango pudding.

- **Blueberries** ranked among the healthiest fruits for years. Now research suggests that in addition to protecting against heart disease and diabetes, they also improve brain function. Another fruit that is great for preschoolers is **cantaloupe**, which provides vitamin C, beta-carotene, bits and pieces of B vitamins, and trace minerals and calcium. Melons are not to be missed when they're plentiful and in season.

Overall, the same healthy foods that adults eat, preschoolers should eat as well. The key is to expose young children to a variety of healthy food choices and then let the child decide what foods they enjoy eating.

Strategy 3: Don't Keep Unhealthy Choices in the House

The food choices parents have been making for their preschool aged children have become alarming. A study done by the Mayo clinic (2016) found that young children now more than any other time in history are consuming too much sodium, saturated fat, and sugar. A FDA study on the eating habits of preschoolers (2017) found about 85 percent of preschoolers consumed a sweetened beverage, a dessert, or a sweet or salty snack three or more times a day!

Foods such as soda, chips, french fries, candy, and fast food are high in salt, saturated fat, and sugar and low in nutrients. Many of these foods also contain bad fats that can increase the risk of childhood obesity and conditions like type 2 diabetes.

Foods that preschoolers should avoid

- **Soda.** This one should be a no-brainer, since hundreds of studies link soda and other sugar-sweetened beverages to obesity, type 2 diabetes, and aggressive behavior in children. Research by Addessi and associates (2005) found that a vast majority of American kids are still chugging these drinks. A twenty-ounce bottle of soda can have over sixty grams of sugar. Some of these drinks have four times what kids should get in an entire day. According to Joan Blake (2016), children just don't have much room in their diets for beverages that supply a ton of empty calories and no nutrients. Many sodas also have caffeine, which children should not have due to the fact caffeine stops the body from absorbing calcium well and can lead to stunted growth.
- **Microwave popcorn.** Up until about three years ago, I had never even heard of perfluorooctanoic acid, or PFOA. It's the chemical used to line the bags of microwave popcorn so that they don't catch on fire. Many studies, including ones by the FDA, the Mayo Clinic, and Ohio State University

show that PFOA has been linked to cancer, postponed puberty, thyroid disease, and high cholesterol in kids. Microwave popcorn is also full of sodium and saturated fat from imitation butter flavor, which is so often found in microwave popcorn. The best alternative is to just pop your own popcorn on the oven or in a popcorn machine.

- **Processed meats.** Meats such as hot dogs, bologna, and other packaged lunch meat may sound like kid-friendly foods, but they are loaded with fat, nitrates, sodium, and preservatives, which can all be harmful to your preschooler's development. These foods have also been found to increase a kid's risk of heart disease, diabetes, and colon cancer. If your child loves lunch meats, opt for preservative-free varieties whenever possible.

- **Cereal.** There is no aisle more attractive to preschoolers than the cereal aisle. "With its rainbow of colors and variety of cartoon characters, sugary kid's cereals are probably some of the most begged for foods in the supermarket," according to Havermans and Jansen (2007). Parents, remember that rainbow-colored bits of oats or rice are not healthy, and no amount of sprayed-on vitamins or extra fiber will make them so. In a recent analysis, *Consumer Reports* (2016) found that only two (Cheerios and Kix) out of fifty kinds of cereal were low enough in sugar and high enough in fiber to be considered good foods for kids.

- **Boxed mac and cheese.** Boxed mac and cheese is highly processed and has little to no nutrients due to the fact it's loaded with sodium and preservatives. The better alternative is to make mac and cheese from scratch, which is simple; just be sure to buy whole-grain pasta, fresh cheese, and any other fresh, not processed ingredients that you and your kids would like to add.

- **Fruit Snacks.** Gummy fruit snacks and fruit rolls are all sugar with no real fruit. Parents should view fruit snacks like candy instead of a nutritional snack. Even though today in many grocery stores, fruit snacks now say "made with real fruit" or "made with real fruit juice," this still does not make them healthy. Most fruit snacks are still packed with as much sugar as a can of soda. If you're looking for an easy snack with some actual nutrition, go with dried real fruit instead.

- **Crackers.** Most parents have some crackers packed away in case their preschooler gets hungry and they're in public with no restaurants in sight. Though the crackers might quiet down a cranky hungry little one, crackers have few nutrients since they are made of processed white flour, preservatives, and unhealthy oils. A better alternative is air popcorn or whole-grain crackers that do not use white flour.

- **Avoid trans fats at all costs.** The worst possible food preschoolers and adults alike can eat are trans fats. Trans fats were developed as a substitute for butter; food manufacturers put vegetable oils through a process called hydrogenation. The addition of hydrogen makes the product firm and resistant to spoilage. However, while hydrogenated or trans fats spread like butter, they also share some of the unwanted properties of saturated fats. They appear to interfere with removing LDL ("bad") cholesterol from the blood and also lower HDL ("good") cholesterol. As a result, foods with trans fats greatly contribute to obesity, heart disease, and certain cancers. Trans fats can be found in many foods preschoolers enjoy, such as fried foods like doughnuts and baked goods including cakes, pie crusts, biscuits, frozen pizza, cookies, crackers, and stick margarines and other spreads. Parents can determine the amount of trans fats in a particular packaged food by looking at the nutrition facts panel. Trans fats are the one food that parents should try to avoid and try to totally cut out of their child's diet.

As a father of three, I know it's almost impossible to completely avoid certain foods and that a preschooler will eventually be exposed to them. These unhealthy foods should never be completely off-limits for children; however, they should be reserved for special occasions such as holidays and birthdays. The key is making sure the foods are not eaten on a regular basis.

Strategy 4: Make Sure Preschoolers Are Getting All Their Proper Vitamins and Minerals

In today's society, many parents do not have the time to cook their preschoolers nutritious, well-balanced meals and opt for fast food. Most of these convenience meals are full of processed food with little nutritional values. Because of this, many pediatricians recommend a daily multivitamin or mineral supplement. I recommend that all parents of preschoolers talk to their child's doctor and get their expert opinion on if they need vitamins, minerals, or maybe another type of food supplement. Your family doctor will be able to give you the proper dose and recommend the proper brands for your child.

Traditionally medical professionals recommend that preschoolers who aren't eating enough food throughout the day or, as stated before, are eating a lot of fast food and processed food should take a vitamin supplement. Preschoolers who do not eat a lot of meat or have a dairy-free diet may need supplements to meet the recommended doses of iron and calcium as well.

Here is a list of the top six vitamins and minerals that preschoolers often need to supplement in their diet:

- Vitamin A promotes normal growth and development; tissue and bone repair; and healthy skin, eyes, and immune responses. Good sources include milk, cheese, eggs, and yellow-to-orange vegetables like carrots, yams, and squash.
- Vitamin B. The family of B vitamins—B2, B3, B6, and B12—aid metabolism, energy production, and healthy circulatory and nervous systems. Good sources include meat, chicken, fish, nuts, eggs, milk, cheese, beans, and soybeans.

- Vitamin C promotes healthy muscles, connective tissue, and skin. Good sources include citrus fruit, strawberries, kiwi, tomatoes, and green vegetables like broccoli.
- Vitamin D promotes bone and tooth formation and helps the body absorb calcium. Good sources include milk and fatty fish like salmon and mackerel. The best source of vitamin D is sunlight.
- Calcium helps build strong bones as a child grows. Good sources include milk, cheese, yogurt, tofu, and calcium-fortified orange juice.
- Iron builds muscle and is essential to healthy red blood cells. Iron deficiency is a risk in adolescence, especially for girls once they begin to menstruate. Good sources include beef and other red meats, turkey, pork, spinach, beans, and prunes.

If your preschoolers are taking vitamins or other supplements, make sure they are well out of reach of children since most taste good and children could easily mistake them as candy. Remember that large doses of vitamins aren't a good idea for children. The fat-soluble vitamins (vitamins A, D, E, and K) can be toxic if kids overdose on excessive amounts. The same goes for iron as well. Your preschooler *can* get too much of a good thing.

Always remember that fresh food is the best source of vitamins and should be the first choice for our preschoolers over giving them nutrients in pill form. Healthy preschoolers get their best start from what you put in your grocery cart, not in the medicine cabinet.

Strategy 5: Let Preschoolers Stop Eating When They're No Longer Hungry, Instead of Insisting That They Clean Their Plates

A study published in the journal *Pediatrics* (2016) found half of all parents expect their adolescent children to clean their plates, while a third prompted them to eat more—even after they stated they were full. There's no reason for parents to provide pressure for preschoolers with normal development and health to clean their plates!

Research suggests that when parents make children clean their plates, they can lose their ability to follow their own hunger cues and to stop eating when they're full. According to a study by the Mayo Clinic in 2016, over time, children forced to clean their plates at every meal may gravitate toward sugary foods and snacks and run the risk of becoming overweight or obese.

In a recent survey, some day-care workers mistakenly believed a clean plate club approach would encourage kids to develop a healthy appetite, Lee Merrit reported in the *Journal of the Academy of Nutrition and Dietetics* (2017). This study also found that childcare providers used controlling feeding practices because of fear of parents' negative reaction if they found that their child did not eat. We as parents must make sure childcare providers, grandparents, and anyone else who is in charge of feeding our children know that it is okay if they choose not to eat or finish their food. Also, we as parents must make sure childcare providers avoid practices such as giving food as a reward and praising preschoolers for cleaning their plates. Dr. Rowell, a childhood feeding specialist, recommends having a conversation with the childcare provider or teacher. She also created a lunch-box card that parents can print, laminate, and put in their child's lunch box that asks teachers not to interfere at mealtime.

The good news is that when children are not forced to clean their plates, they become healthier later in life. Dr. Amber Goldwater, a researcher at the University of Minnesota (2016), for instance, have found that preschoolers who were not forced to clean their plates grew up to be young adults who used the internal cues of hunger and fullness to guide their eating habits. These young adults who followed internal cues on hunger not only had a lower body mass index than those who used external cues, but they also had lowered instances of disordered eating.

Strategy 6: Involve Kids in Menu Planning, Shopping, and Cooking

The act of involving preschoolers in the process of planning, shopping, and cooking what they should eat is an important step in raising healthy eaters. The menu planning process can mean sampling, giving your child a choice of what healthy foods they would like to eat. An example of this could be having the child pick chicken or fish, brown rice or sweet potatoes, or carrots or beans. According to Amanda Nunez of the American Council for healthy eating, by allowing children to make choices, they can have ownership over what they put into their bodies.

The second step in preschool involvement is going to the grocery store with them. The shopping trip should be an interactive experience where you as the parent point out the healthy foods your child can choose for the meals they are going to eat. During this time as a parent, we can point out how to tell if fruits and vegetables are ripe or not and what the best cuts of meat are. Remember, this should be a time to talk about healthy food options, not just a quick run through aisles where the parent puts stuff in the cart and then quickly checks out.

The third step in preschool food involvement is preparation and cooking. Have your preschooler perform age-appropriate tasks such as washing the produce, measuring and dumping in ingredients, and stirring and mixing. Once the food is prepared, then allow for your child to watch as you bake, steam, or cook the food. The cooking part is usually not age-appropriate; however, with close supervision, they should be allowed to watch the food cook.

Children who attend day care can use the involvement method by parents making lists of what items are available for different parts of their lunches and having them choose from the items when parents pack their lunches or snacks. Preschoolers should know they need an entree item, at least one fruit, a vegetable, and a healthy snack. Cross items out when they are used or you run out, and then repeat the choosing and shopping process.

Now, I'm not suggesting you give your preschoolers executive control over grocery shopping and meal planning. Instead, I'm suggesting that you start with once-a-week involvement and then move to two or three meals. Having kids involved in the meal planning and preparation process does take more time and effort, but in the long run, it will be well worth it for the long-term habits that will be learned and then passed down to other generations.

Strategy 7: Eat Together as a Family as Often as Possible; Make Mealtime Family Time

Sadly, Americans rarely eat together anymore. In fact, according to a 2017 study by healthy kids.gov, the average American eats one in every five meals in their car, one in four Americans eats at least one fast-food meal every single day, and over 80 percent of American families report eating a single meal together less than five days a week. It's tragic that so many Americans are missing out on what could be meaningful time with their preschoolers, and the fact is that not eating together also has quantifiably negative effects both physically and psychologically on children.

According to a study by Michael Cambridge (2015), children who do not eat dinner with their parents at least twice a week were 40 percent more likely to be overweight compared to those who do. On the other hand, children who do eat dinner with their parents four or more days a week have less trouble with drugs and alcohol, eat healthier, show better academic performance, and report being closer with their parents than children who eat dinner with their parents less often, according to a study conducted by the National Center on Addiction and Substance Abuse at Columbia University (2014).

The good news is that children who eat regular family dinners also consume more fruits, vegetables, vitamins, and micronutrients, as well as fewer fried foods and soft drinks. And the nutritional benefits keep paying dividends even after kids grow up: young adults who ate regular family meals as teens are less likely to be obese and more likely to eat healthily once they live on their own. Research by the U.S. Department of Agriculture (2016) has even found a connection between regular family dinners and the reduction in symptoms of medical disorders such as asthma. The benefit might be due to two possible byproducts of a shared family meal: lower anxiety and the chance to check in about a child's medication compliance.

It isn't just the presence of healthy foods that leads to all these benefits. The dinner atmosphere is also important. Parents need to be warm and engaged, rather than controlling and restrictive, to encourage healthy eating in their children. When parents have dinner conversation with their children, not only will they be healthier and happier but also smarter.

Family meals = smarter kids

Research by Shanon Bream (2017) found that for young children, dinnertime conversation boosts vocabulary even more than being read aloud to. The researchers counted the number of rare words—those not found on a list of three thousand most common words—that the families used during dinner conversation. Young kids learned one thousand rare words at the dinner table, compared to only 143 from parents reading storybooks aloud. Kids who have a large vocabulary read earlier and more easily.

A study by the National Association for Healthy Children (2015) found a consistent association between family dinner frequency and academic performance. Adolescents who ate family meals five to seven times a week were twice as likely to get *A*s in school as those who ate dinner with their families fewer than two times a week.

Remember, the real power of dinners lies in their interpersonal quality. If family members sit in stony silence, if parents yell at each other or scold their kids, family dinner won't confer positive benefits. Sharing a healthy dinner won't magically transform parent-child relationships. According to Anne Fishel, author of *The Family Dinner Project*, dinner may be the one time of the day when a parent and child can share a positive experience—a well-cooked meal, a joke, or a story—and these small moments can gain momentum to create stronger connections away from the table.

CHAPTER 3

DEALING WITH PICKY EATERS

Even the most nutritious meal will have no positive effects on your preschooler if he or she won't eat it. Some preschoolers are just picky eaters, and this makes it more challenging to ensure they are eating the proper foods all the time. This chapter will give some common examples of what parents may be dealing with, along with some strategies to help ensure preschoolers get all the nutrients they need to be healthy.

When Do Toddlers Become Picky Eaters?

According to Adina Pearson, the author of the Healthy Little Eaters blog (2017), picky eating can be a natural part of your child's development as kids' growth spurts start to slow and they begin to test their autonomy and boundaries. It can begin as early as eighteen months, but kids typically become selective about what they eat between the ages of two and five.

Part of coping with your child's behavioral shift, Pearson states, is to manage expectations. "At that point, they might even reject foods they used to like," Pearson says. "Parents need to expect that around preschool age kids are going to start rejecting some things."

What Causes Picky Eaters?

There are a number of reasons why preschoolers might become picky eaters. Some of the most common causes of picky eating are the following:

- **An instinct for self-preservation.** Some studies suggest that kids' rejection of new foods—particularly leafy greens and bitter vegetables—is actually an evolutionary survival mechanism to keep small children from sampling poisonous plants, stemming all the way back to our hunter-gatherer days.
- **A slowdown in growth.** From birth to age two, children undergo extraordinary growth, and when that growth rate naturally slows, so does the toddler's appetite. According to Bourcier and associates (2003), parents often misinterpret this dip in food consumption as picky eating.
- **A need for independence.** As kids enter the toddler phase, there's an increased desire for autonomy, and exerting control over food is one of the easiest ways to claim some independence.
- **A tendency to pick up bad habits.** A 2002 Ohio State University study along with research by Dr. Frank Adams, Florida A&M (2014) have shown that the eating habits of caregivers and even peers have a noticeable impact on how and what kids eat. The more they see those around them refusing to try new foods or maintaining unhealthy eating habits, the more likely they'll mimic those behaviors.
- **A medical issue.** There could also be medical and physiological reasons behind your child's picky eating habits, including tongue tie (in which the connecting skin under the tongue is too short); poor oral motor skills (like trouble chewing or swallowing); gastrointestinal trouble; sensitivities to textures, smells, and flavors; and anxiety disorder and autism, to name a few. It's always worth checking in with your doctor if you have concerns about your child's picky eating.

Identify What Your Preschooler's Picky Foods Are

One of the first steps to helping your preschooler become a less picky eater is to identify the foods they are not interested in eating. Many times preschoolers do not like a food based on things such as color, texture, or even the taste of the food.

According to Wardle (2003)**,** as humans, we're designed to prefer sweet foods and dislike bitter ones. Sweet equals survival—think breast milk—and bitter may mean something's toxic. Some foods might register as a big "yuck" with your preschooler because they actually have more taste buds than you do (we lose them as we age), so the flavor of foods is amplified for little ones. Your child could also be genetically wired to be more sensitive to bitter foods, as research clearly shows some kids are.

Many preschoolers simply will not eat certain foods based on colors. A study by Mennella and associates (2008)_found, that children were more disgusted by green food, with almost half of youngsters admitting they have refused to eat something on their plate simply because of its color. Children also found black, blue, and purple foods all off-putting (see table 3).

Table 1. Top ten colors children found most off-putting for food

1. Green
2. Black
3. Purple
4. Blue
5. Brown
6. Beige
7. Pink
8. Red
9. Yellow
10. Orange

Dr. Megan Arroll (2016), research has shown children demonstrate the most positive emotional reactions, such as happiness and excitement, towards bright colors and this survey supports this as children's most popular food colors included red, yellow and orange. When dealing with a picky preschool eater keep in mind color and try to add bright foods such as fruits to their diet."

If it's a texture issue making your preschooler a picky eater, then exploring different ways to make certain ingredients more appealing might be worth the effort. For example, the texture of a perfectly ripe avocado cut into cubes is very different from avocados mashed into guacamole.

If your preschooler does not like different ingredients mixed together or touching, consider preparing their meals deconstructed. For example, if you were preparing a sandwich, give your preschooler the bread, cheese, meat, and toppings all on the side, and let them make it their own personal way. Another idea for dealing with children who are sensitive about food touching: you can invest in plates that have dividers to keep each item separated.

Strategies That Can Help Combat the Picky-Eating Preschooler

Over the years many strategies have been used by parents to combat picky eaters. The following section details some of the more successful and unique ideas that can be used to ensure your preschooler is eating properly.

Strategy 1: Take a taste

Insist on the taking-a-bite-before-saying-you-don't-like-something rule. There are many variations on this tasting strategy. Some people go with one big bite; others say try three small bites. There is also a game where a roll of the dice determines how many bites to take. I recommend going with whatever works best for your preschooler. The key is that they are at least trying the food.

Strategy 2: Give the preschooler choices

Once a week; let your picky-eating preschooler plan the menu. This is a chance to give them some control over the meal. Let them pick the types of food service along with the portion size as long as the take-a-taste rule is still in play.

Strategy 3: Present new foods several times

It takes time for preschoolers to get used to something new. According to Dr. Orlene Kerek (2008), "Kids (and adults) need to try something 10–15 times before they get used to eating a new food. (pg 114-121)" This can be a long, frustrating process, but it's much quicker than pressuring them to eat it and them refusing for the next twenty years.

Parents must keep presenting preschoolers with healthy foods they like and continue to give them the opportunity to try new things. Be sure to prepare the new food for adults only to eat, and your preschooler can try the food only if they want.

Strategy 4: Pair new foods with known favorite foods

Another strategy that can be used is to try deceiving your preschooler's palate by pairing new foods with the flavors they love. Researchers tested this idea by presenting kids with a choice of two kinds of chips—one familiar and one new. In addition, some kids were offered a familiar chip dip. Others were offered an unfamiliar chip dip. The kids who had access to the familiar dip were more likely to try tasting the new chips (Pliner and Stallberg-White 2000).

Along similar lines, studies show that kids are more likely to accept a new food—even a bitter or sour food—if their first exposure to it is paired with sweetness. In one experiment, young children lost their aversion to bitter grapefruit juice if it was initially mixed with extra sugar (Capaldi and Privitera 2008).

In another experiment, researchers gave kids sweetened vegetables on a number of occasions and then asked the kids to taste and rate the vegetables in their natural, unsweetened state. The kids reported an increased liking for the unsweetened versions of the vegetables (Havermans and Jansen 2007).

Best foods for picky eaters to pair with new favorites

Since preschoolers can be picky in their own unique way and that can even vary from meal to meal, it can be hard to figure out what to feed picky eaters. However, there are certain types of foods most kids tend to enjoy, especially since you can customize them to your kids' tastes. Plus, they're wonderful vehicles for hiding (and therefore introducing) new flavors. These foods include the following:

- smoothies
- meatballs
- pancakes
- muffins

Remember, at the end of the day, you want to try to get your picky eaters accustomed to the foods your family often eats.

Always remember that if you are concerned about your preschooler's picky-eating habits, talk with your pediatrician, who can help troubleshoot and make sure your child is getting all the necessary nutrients to grow and develop. Also keep in mind that picky eating usually is a normal developmental stage for most preschoolers. All we can do as parents is our best to patiently guide them on their path toward healthy eating.

CHAPTER 4

SEVEN DAYS OF SAMPLE MENUS

A healthy meal plan consists of breakfast, lunch, dinner, and one or two healthy snacks. Because your preschooler is growing and developing, three healthy meals a day are especially important.

The example meal plans in this chapter are based on the ideas from throughout this book and are just suggestions. Always remember if you have any questions about the proper nutrition for your child, please consult your pediatrician or family dietitian.

Sample Menu 1 **Breakfast**	Breakfast sandwich of • Whole-grain bread • Egg • Ham • Tomato slices Skim or 1 percent milk
Morning Snack	Yogurt Strawberries Water

Lunch	Homemade chicken strips
	Carrot and celery sticks with salad dressing for dipping
	Milk
Afternoon Snack	Apple slices
	Cheese stick
	Water
Dinner	Mini meatballs
	Whole wheat pasta with tomato and vegetable pasta sauce
	Milk

Sample Menu 2

Breakfast	Cheerios cereal with milk
	Strawberries and banana slices
	Cranberry juice
Morning Snack	Fresh or canned mango or peach slices
	Cottage cheese
	Water
Lunch	Mini cheese and chicken quesadilla
	Cucumber slices with salad dressing for dipping
	Orange wedges
	Milk

Afternoon Snack	Fruit smoothie
	Peanut butter on celery with raisins
	Water
Dinner	Beef and broccoli stir-fry
	Brown rice
	Milk

Sample Menu 3

Breakfast	Fruity breakfast parfaits of
	• Blueberries
	• Strawberries
	• Yogurt
	Sprinkle granola on top
	Skim or 1 percent milk
Morning Snack	Cheese and crackers
	Water
Lunch	Pizza-stuffed zucchini with
	• Zucchini
	• Pepperoni
	• Mozzarella cheese
	• Marinara sauce
	Milk
Afternoon Snack	Bran muffin mini bites
	Water

Dinner	Ground beef and pasta skillet
	Applesauce
	Milk

Sample Menu 4

Breakfast	Whole wheat toast
	Blueberries
	Banana slices
	Milk
Morning Snack	Homemade yogurt pops
	Water
Lunch	Apple and cheese wrapped in ham
	Sweet potato chips
	Milk
Afternoon Snack	Mini fruit pizza
	Water
Dinner	Loaded twice-baked potato with
	• Potatoes
	• Lean meat
	• Broccoli
	• Cheese
	Milk

Sample Menu 5

Breakfast	Blueberry pie oatmeal
	• Oatmeal
	• Blueberries
	• Honey
	Skim or 1 percent milk
Morning Snack	Homemade trail mix
	Water
Lunch	Lunch kebabs
	• Deli turkey
	• Cubed cheese
	• Wheat bread cut in cubes
	• Tomato slices
	Milk
Afternoon Snack	Orange cranberry muffin
	Water
Dinner	Chicken fajitas
	Chips with mild salsa
	Milk

Sample Menu 6

Breakfast	Whole wheat pancakes
	Sliced banana
	Milk

Dr. Jon Kester

Morning Snack	Dried apricotsString cheese Water
Lunch	Tuna salad sandwich on wheat bread Cucumber slices with salad dressing for dipping Milk
Afternoon Snack	Homemade popsicles made with 100 percent fruit juice Water
Dinner	Chicken and vegetable stir-fry Brown rice Milk

Sample Menu 7

Breakfast	Breakfast burrito bites of • Ham • Cooked egg • Rolled in a whole wheat tortilla • Cut crossways like sushi Skim or 1 percent milk
Morning Snack	Homemade trail mix Water
Lunch	Hamburgers Baked sweet potato fries Milk

30

Afternoon Snack	Apple slices
	Water
Dinner	Mini whole-grain pizza
	• Whole-grain crust
	• Pizza sauce
	• Low-fat mozzarella cheese
	• Lean beef or chicken topping
	Milk

CHAPTER 5

CONCLUSION

How your preschooler eats today will have a striking impact on their health throughout adolescence and adulthood. Consuming nutritious foods helps children grow, develop, do well academically, and feel good about themselves. Good nutrition also helps prevent preschoolers from having issues such as eating disorders, obesity, dental cavities, and iron-deficiency anemia later in life. Teaching children the importance of good nutrition throughout childhood will lay the foundation for a healthier, more fulfilling life.

Remember that preschoolers require a variety of nutrient-dense foods such as fresh fruits, vegetables, whole grains, meat, and fish and adequate calories in order to grow and develop properly. It's crucial that your preschooler is consuming the essential nutrients they need to grow. Preschoolers who eat healthy have many benefits such as the following:

- stabilized energy throughout the day
- improved minds
- evened-out moods
- a healthy weight
- no mental health conditions, such as depression, anxiety, and ADHD

Healthy eating habits are more likely to stay with you if you learn them as a preschooler according to research by Nicklaus (2009). That's why it's important that you teach your children good habits now in their preschool years.

Things from This Book to Consider

There are an unlimited number of tips available on how to get your preschooler to eat nutritious food. Above all, the best way to help your child with nutrition is to encourage healthy habits.

- **Be a role model.** Kids eat the way you eat. Follow these tips yourself, and your child will be more likely to eat that way too.
- **Start them young.** Food preferences develop early in life. Expose your child to different kinds of food early on, and continue as they grow older.
- **Focus on overall diet.** Instead of focusing on specific foods, focus on eating patterns. Provide as much whole, minimally processed food as you can. Avoid packaged and processed food when you can.
- **Know what they should be eating.** Much of the focus is placed on what we should avoid. This can lead to feeling deprived. Instead, focus on what you and your child *should* be eating. This keeps eating healthy as a positive action.
- **Don't force them to eat.** Don't make your child clean their plate. They need to learn to listen to their bodies. When they feel full and are allowed to stop eating, they are less likely to overeat.
- **Skip the food reward.** When you use food as a reward or to show affection, your child could start using food to cope with their emotions. Instead, give them hugs, praise, attention, or time together.
- **Set snack boundaries.** Teach your child to ask before having a snack. Have him or her sit at the table to eat the snack, not in front of the TV. Put snacks like pretzels or

popcorn on a plate or in a bowl; don't let your child eat directly out of the bag.

Hopefully the information that you read in this book will help your preschooler eat well and grow up healthy. Young children need our help as parents to develop healthy eating and physical activity habits for life.

Remember, the information from this book needs to be used as a reference. During your child's early years, you and your preschooler's doctor must be partners in maintaining your child's health; the doctor should always be consulted before making any type of major nutritional decisions. I believe that the best way to grow healthy preschoolers is by working with a team of experts who all have your children's best interest in mind. I recommend working closely with health-care professionals and other parents and teachers to get the most effective nutrition information that will allow your preschooler to develop healthy habits for life.

References

Addessi, E., A. T. Galloway, E. Visalberghi, and L. L. Birch. 2005. "Specific Social Influences on the Acceptance of Novel Foods in 2–5-Year-Old Children." *Appetite* 45(3):264–71.

Batsell, W. R., A. S. Brown, A. E. Ansfield, and G. Y. Paschall. 2002. "You Will Eat All of That!: A Retrospective Analysis of Forced Consumption Episodes." *Appetite* 38(3):211–219.

Bevelander, K. E., D. J. Anschütz, and R. C. Engels. 2012. "The Effect of a Fictitious Peer on Young Children's Choice of Familiar v. Unfamiliar Low- and High-Energy-Dense Foods." *Br J Nutr* 108(6):1126–33.

Birch, L. L., L. McPhee, B. C. Shoba, E. Pirok, and L. Steinberg. 1987. "What Kind of Exposure Reduces Children's Food Neophobia? Looking vs. Tasting." *Appetite* 9(3):171–8.

Bourcier, E., D. J. Bowen, H. Meischke, and C. Moinpour. 2003. "Evaluation of Strategies Used by Family Food Preparers to Influence Healthy Eating." *Appetite* 41(3):265–272.

Bream, Shanon. 2017. "Preschoolers' Nutritional Needs in the 21st Century." *Journal of Health and Wellness* 57(2):111–8.

Brown, K. A., J. Ogden, C. Vögele, and E. L. Gibson. 2008. "The Role of Parental Control Practices in Explaining Children's Diet and BMI." *Appetite* 50(2–3):252–9.

Busick, D. B., J. Brooks, S. Pernecky, R. Dawson, and J. Petzoldt. 2008. "Parent Food Purchases as a Measure of Exposure and Preschool-Aged Children's Willingness to Identify and Taste Fruit and Vegetables." *Appetite* 51, no. 3(November): 468–73.

Cambridge, Michael. 2015. "Variety Is the Spice of Life: Strategies for Promoting Fruit and Vegetable Acceptance in Infants." *Physiology and Behavior* 94:29–38.

Capaldi, E. D., and G. J. Privitera. 2008. "Decreasing Dislike for Sour and Bitter in Children and Adults." *Appetite* 50(1):139–45.

Centers for Disease Control and Prevention. 2017. "Annual Report." Retrieved September 21, 2017, from http://usdcop.gov/annual report2017/display.asp?id=16.

Fishel, A. K. 2015. *Home for Dinner Mixing, Food, Fun, and Conversation for a Happier Family and Healthier Kids.* Saranac Lake, NY: AMACOM.

Fisher, J. O., and L. L. Birch. 1999. "Restricting Access to Palatable Foods Affects Children's Behavioral Response, Food Selection, and Intake." *Am J Clin Nutr* 69(6):1264–72.

Florida Healthy Kids. 2017. Retrieved from https://healthykids.org/.

Frazier, B. N., S. A. Gelman, N. Kaciroti, J. W. Russell, and J. C. Lumeng. 2012. "I'll Have What She's Having: The Impact of Model Characteristics on Children's Food Choices." *Dev Sci*, no. 1, 87–98.

Galloway, J.E. 2006. "'Finish Your Soup' Counterproductive Effects of Pressuring Children to Eat on Intake and Affect." *Appetite* 46(3):318–23.

Havermans, R. C., and A. Jansen. 2007. "Increasing Children's Liking of Vegetables through Flavour-Flavour Learning." *Appetite* 48(2):259–62.

Health, Department of Health and Human Services. 2015. Lincoln, NE: Nebraska Department of Health and Human Services.

Hughes, S. O., H. Patrick, T. G. Power, J. O. Fisher, C. B. Anderson, and T. A. Nicklas. 2007. "The Impact of Child Care Providers' Feeding on Children's Food Consumption." *J Dev Behav Pediatr* 28(2):100–7.

Kerek, Orlene. 2008. "High 5 for Kids: The Impact of a Home Visiting Program on Fruit and Vegetable Intake of Parents and Their Preschool Children." *Prev Med* 47(1):77–8.

Loewen, R., and P. Pliner. 1999. "Effects of Prior Exposure to Palatable and Unpalatable Novel Foods on Children's Willingness to Taste Other Novel Foods." *Appetite* 32(3):351–66.

Mayo Clinic. *Children Obesity Study.* 2016. New York: Time Books.

Nanney, M. S., S. Johnson, M. Elliott, and D. Haire-Joshu. 2007. "Frequency of Eating Homegrown Produce Is Associated with Higher Intake among Parents and Their Preschool-Aged Children in Rural Missouri." *J Am Diet Assoc* 107(4):577–84.

National Association Healthy Children. January 12, 2015. "Annual Children's Health and Wellness Study." Retrieved January 21, 2017, from http://Nahc.org/annualreport2015/display.asp?id=16.

Nicklaus, S. 2009. "Development of Food Variety in Children." *Appetite* 52(1):253–5.

Pearson, Adina. 2017 Healthy Little Eaters blog, http://healthylittle eaters.com/.

Pliner, P., and C. Stallberg-White. 2000. "'Pass the Ketchup, Please': Familiar Flavors Increase Children's Willingness to Taste Novel Foods." *Appetite* 34(1):95–103.

Rozin, P. 1976. "The Selection of Foods by Rats, Humans, and Other Animals." In *Advances in the Study of Behavior (Volume 6)*, edited by J. Rosenblatt, R. A. Hinde, C. Beer, and E. Shaw, 125-133. New York: Academic Press.

Sellen, D. W. 2001. "Comparison of Infant Feeding Patterns Reported for Nonindustrial Populations with Current Recommendations." *Journal of Nutrition* 131:2707–15.

Terras, S. 1994. *Stress, How Your Diet Can Help: The Practical Guide to Positive Health Using Diet, Vitamins, Minerals, Herbs and Amino Acids.* Thorsons.

U.S. Consumer Report. 2016. "The Best Food for Your Children: 2016—Detailed Tables [Data Tables]." Retrieved from http://www.usconsumer.com/hhes/socdemo/education/data/2016/tables.html.

USDA Dietary Guidelines for Americans. 2017. New York: Skyhorse Publishing.

U.S. Department of Agriculture. 2016, January 1. "Children's Health and Wellness Study." Retrieved January 21, 2017, from http://usda.gov/fastfacts/display.asp?id=16.

Wansink, B., D. R. Just, C. R. Payne, and M. Klinger. 2012. "Attractive Names Sustain Increased Vegetable Intake in Schools." *Preventive Medicine* 55(4):330–2.

Wardle, J., L. J. Cooke, E. L. Gibson, M. Sapochnik, A. Sheiham, and M. Lawson. 2003a. "Increasing Children's Acceptance of Vegetables; A Randomized Trial of Parent-Led Exposure." *Appetite* 40(2):155–62.

Wardle, J., M. L. Herrera, L. Cooke, and E. L. Gibson. 2003b. "Modifying Children's Food Preferences: The Effects of Exposure and Reward on Acceptance of an Unfamiliar Vegetable." *Eur J Clin Nutr* 57(2):341–8.

Wardle, J., S. Carnell, and L. Cooke. 2005. "Parental Control over Feeding and Children's Fruit and Vegetable Intake: How Are They Related? *J Am Diet Assoc* 105(2):227–32.

Werbach, M. R. 1989. *Nutritional Influences on Illness: A Source Book of Clinical Research* Thorsons.

ABOUT THE AUTHOR

Dr. Jon Kester is a highly-established teacher, author, and a strong advocate for family values. He has more than 20 years of diverse, well-rounded experience in the fields of fitness and nutrition; Kester's qualifications include a Doctorate in Education from Edgewood College, a Master's of Science in Exercise and Sports Science from the University of Wisconsin – Lacrosse as well as two bachelor's degrees from Winona State University. During his studies he was able to explore the health benefits of proper diets on people of all ages. Dr. Kester then applied his research to help countless numbers of people live a healthier and happier life.

Though Dr. Kester values his education, he feels that his best experience comes from being a stay at home dad. Dr. Kester's greatest desire is being the best dad possible to his three children. One way that he can do so is by making sure his kids are eating healthy. Dr. Kester has spent copious hours doing research to insure that his kids are consuming nutritious foods which will help them grow, develop, and feel good about themselves. He loves to share information with the world though his writing of books and articles and plans to continue help fellow parents any way he can.

Printed in the United States
By Bookmasters